West Coast Border Steam

Peter J. Robinson

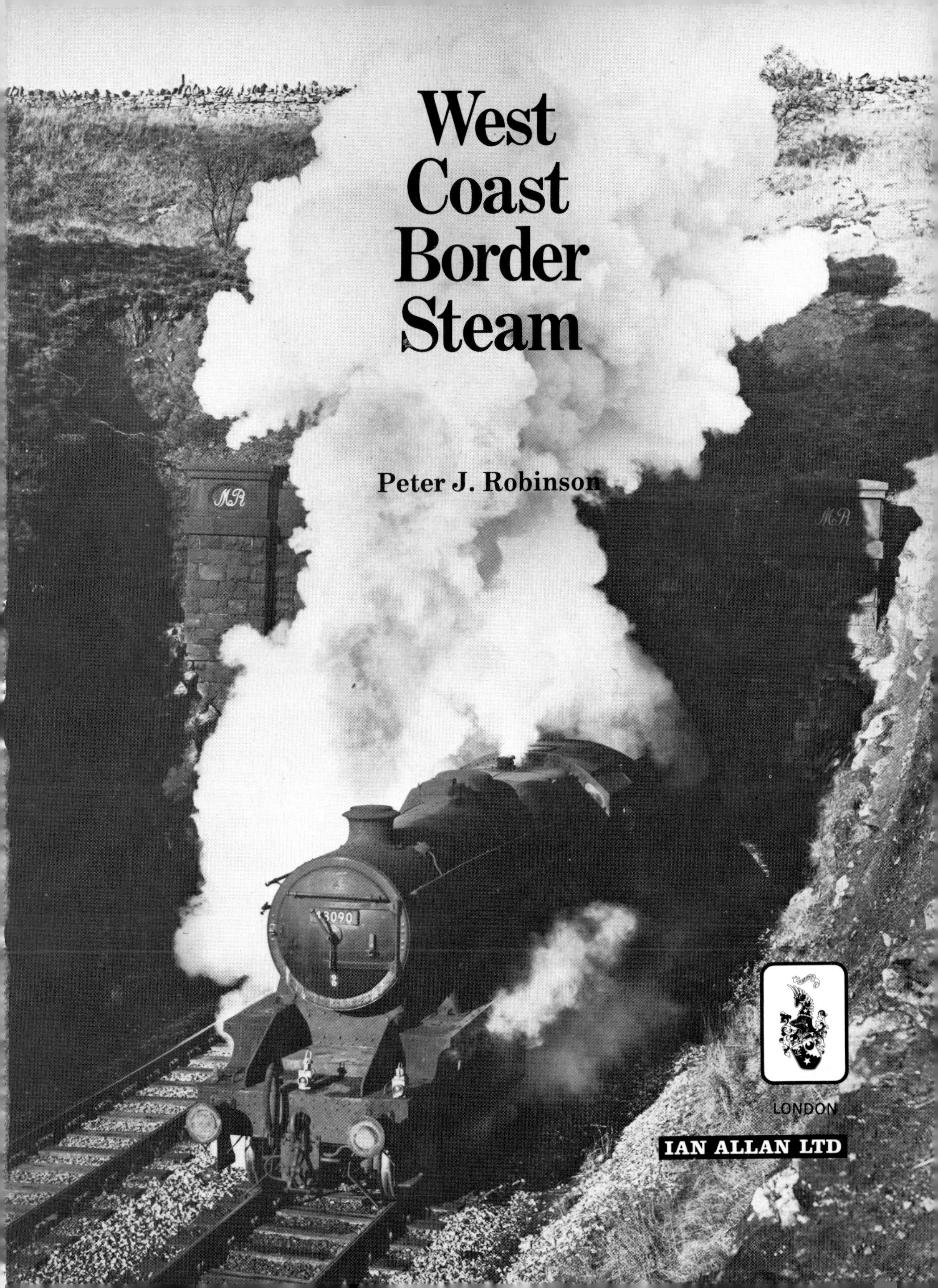

LONDON

IAN ALLAN LTD

First published 1977

ISBN 0 7110 0782 9

Published by Ian Allan Ltd, Shepperton, Surrey, and printed in the United Kingdom by Ian Allan Printing Ltd.

Introduction

My first experience of the fascination of Carlisle for the ferro-equinologist was in the early 1950s, when I was a schoolboy living in Hexham. My parents allowed me to spend 7s 6d of my pocket money on a North Eastern Region 'Runabout ticket', which afforded me unlimited rail travel for seven days in an area bounded by Berwick, Carlisle, Penrith (via Darlington), York and Scarborough (via Whitby). Thus on the first day (a Monday) of my ticket I boarded the 7.20 a.m. stopping train to Carlisle, where I stayed in the Citadel station until returning home on the 7.00 p.m. to Hexham.

So much did I enjoy my day in Carlisle that I used my ticket to make six further visits to Carlisle and went nowhere else! Not only did this week introduce me to Carlisle's attractions as a railway centre, but also to the warmth and kindness of its people — especially the railwaymen.

The 7.00 p.m. from Carlisle to Newcastle was worked by an engine and men from the ex-North British Railway Canal shed, often using a Scottish engine between turns from and to Edinburgh by the Waverley Route. On the Tuesday evening the appearance of the same smut-covered schoolboy who had travelled on the train the previous evening was sufficiently noteworthy to the engine crew of A3 No 60068 *Sir Visto* that I was invited on to the footplate. Suffice it to say that for the following five days I returned home on the engine, being smuggled on at the last minute before departure and jumping off at Hexham behind a screen of steam from the injector overflow. On the Sunday I returned on the locomotive with a different crew and although I was unaware of the rarity, the engine was V4 No 61701 (popularly known as 'Bantam Hen') from Eastfield depot in Glasgow.

Further clear memories of this formative visit are the extreme clarity of the station announcements (made from the signalbox in

the heart of the station) and the prodigious length of the trains. Immediately the Stanier Pacific on the afternoon Birmingham Scotch express had drawn to a stand the announcement would be:

"This is Carlisle, Carlisle Citadel, Carlisle. The train now standing at this platform, platform number three, is the 11 o'clock from Birmingham. This train will go forward at 3.48 to Carstairs. From Carstairs the train will be divided. The front ten coaches will go forward to Glasgow Central, calling at Motherwell, the rear seven coaches are for Edinburgh Princes Street. Carstairs will be the first stop".

Seventeen Coaches! How are the mighty fallen!

A further scripted announcement presaged the passage of a spotless Polmadie or Camden 'Princess Coronation' on the 'Royal Scot', as follows:

'The train now approaching platform 3 will not call at this station. Passengers stand well clear'

Little did I know that, unlike the corres-

The last regular turn on the West Coast main line for an ex-LMS passenger engine. 'Jubilee' 4-6-0 No 45627 (formerly *Sierra Leone*) passes Brisco with the 14.00 Glasgow Central to Liverpool in July 1966.

ponding 'Capitals Limited' on the East Coast Route, the 'Royal Scot' was not non-stop, but called at Kingmoor in the down direction and Upperby in the up to change crews.

Another highlight would be the arrival of the 9.00 a.m. from Perth to Euston which was handed over by two 'Black Fives' — the leading one from Carstairs and the train engine from Perth with Highland Line tablet apparatus — to an Upperby 'Princess Coronation'.

Whilst I lost no opportunity to make further visits to Carlisle, it was much later when I discovered that not only was Carlisle itself a compelling railway centre, but that virtually all the lines converging upon it were remarkable in themselves.

Clockwise from the North the first line we come across is the ex-North British Railway Waverley Route to Edinburgh, with the

lengthy severe climbs in each direction to Whitrope Summit and the uniquely isolated railway community of Riccarton Junction, where the Border Counties branch from Hexham trailed in from the South. The Waverley Route leaves Carlisle in a westerly direction and boxes three points of the compass before crossing the northbound Caledonian line in an easterly direction at Kingmoor. From this line the Silloth branch meandered west along the south bank of the Solway in its coverted waterway basin from Canal Junction and the rural Langholm branch forked off west at Riddings Junction, just over the Scottish Border.

Above: 'Britannia' Pacific No 70038 *Robin Hood* on a Glasgow to Liverpool train slows for a signal check at Harrisons Sidings, Shap, due to the failure of No 45072 on a preceding Glasgow to Morecambe train at Shap summit in July 1967.

Below: 'Britannia' Pacific No 70013 coasts into Penrith with the Workington portion of the 'Lakes Express', passing Class 2 2-6-0 No 46426 waiting to back on to the rear of the train to take it on via Keswick to Workington.

Next, the ex-North Eastern line turns east from the south end of Citadel station with a severe eastbound climb to the watershed near Brampton Junction. From this line at Petteril Bridge Junction there branches arguably the most dramatic of all routes to Carlisle — the

Settle and Carlisle to Hellifield and the West Riding. The superb scenery with impressive stone viaducts and tunnels punctuating the southbound climb to Ais Gill and northbound to Blea Moor showed steam engines hard at work in some of the most impressive locations in Great Britain.

Next in a clockwise direction, the Lancaster and Carlisle line comes in from the south, trains having negotiated the superb Lune Gorge, then the steep climb to Shap Summit followed by a curving pastoral descent of 30 miles to Carlisle, which was a formidable obstacle for southbound trains starting cold from Carlisle. This is Carlisle's

Above: A fine example of Upperby cleaning. 'Duchess' 4-6-2 No 46238 *City of Carlisle* attempts to boost the efforts of Carlisle United against Preston North End to reach the quarter-finals of the FA Cup. The magnificently prepared engine is seen taking a run at Shap over the relatively level stretch between Penrith and Clifton with a 14coach football special on 15 February 1964. Alas, Carlisle lost 1-0!

Below: Until 1967 both Thrimby Grange starting signals were LNW-design lower quadrants. 'Britannia' Pacific No 70010 *Owen Glendower* is seen here passing this antique pair with the 14.00 Glasgow to Liverpool in July 1966.

main artery and the full range of modern LMS and British Railways designs could be seen tackling at speed the heavy gradients with maximum loads.

At Penrith the Cockermouth, Keswick & Penrith line branches off the Shap route over formidable gradients to Keswick, whence it pursues a more leisurely course, initially alongside Bassenthwaite Lake to Workington, which can be reached more directly by the relatively featureless ex-Furness Railway route from Carlisle.

The remaining lines radiating from Carlisle all leave on the same ex-Caledonian metals as far as Gretna Junction, where the Glasgow &

Left: Against the background of the gently rounded Howgill hills, Class 5 4-6-0 No 44971 and 2-6-4T banker No 42251 get to grips with the Shap climb at Greenholme, soon after leaving Tebay with the afternoon Crewe to Carlisle parcels train in April 1967.

Below left: Rounding the curve at Wreay, rebuilt 'Patriot' 4-6-0 No 45531 *Sir Frederick Harrison* seems to be struggling with a Barry Links to Liverpool troop special in August 1963.

Below: 'Jubilee' 4-6-0 No 45721 *Impregnable* comes roaring strongly under the A6 road bridge past Harrison's Lime Works with the 14.00 Glasgow to Liverpool in July 1965. Despite its bedraggled appearance this engine was running well ahead of time and making a spirited climb with its 13coach load.

Duchess Pacific No 46250 *City of Lichfield* leaves a sizeable vapour trail in the cold December air as it climbs towards Southwaite with the up 'Royal Scot' in 1962.

South Western route to Glasgow via Dumfries leaves in a westerly direction. This line runs along the flat Solway plain to the redstone town of Dumfries, where the highly scenic route to Stranraer via Castle Douglas climbs west in an impressive manner to Lochanhead, before running through very bleak and inhospitable country over the Water of Fleet viaducts.

Finally, the other northbound route from Gretna Junction is the ex-Caledonian continuation of the West Coast route with heavy climbs to Beattock Summit, especially from the south, on which, like Shap, crack trains had the benefit of the best motive power.

In Carlisle each of the lines mentioned had its own yard and engine sheds and even into the 1960s retained its own personality. Although the individuality was progressively reduced by closures and amalgamation of all freight traffic in the vast Kingmoor marshalling yard and consequent concentration of locomotive facilities at Kingmoor and Upperby, this did not at the time affect the various architectural styles and lineside furniture characteristics which made the different routes to Carlisle all distinctive.

I hope that the photographs in this book show adequately the variety of motive power and scenery on the lines converging on and in Carlisle even in the last decade of steam traction. May the book give readers as much pleasure as I have had in taking the pictures.

Peter Robinson

North Shields

46250

45350

Left: Despite leaking steam from nearly every pore, Class 5 4-6-0 No 45350 makes a strong climb past Thrimby Grange soon after sunrise in September 1967 with a heavily loaded Carlisle to Wigan Bamfurlong Class 7 freight. At the rear of the train can be seen the Thrimby Grange home signal, a lower-quadrant LNW type, which survived until replaced by the electric signalling during electrification.

Above: Running-in from Crewe works, Class 5 4-6-0 No 45247 of Rhyl depot hurries past Wreay North with the Edinburgh-Birmingham train, running independently of the Glasgow portion in the freezing fog of Christmas Eve 1962.

Below: 'Duchess' Pacific No 46250 *City of Lichfield* gets into its stride at the start of the climb to Shap summit with the 9.00 Perth to Euston in March 1963. Seen here passing Wreay North, the engine would work through to Euston on this train.

Above: A rare visitor to Carlisle. The unique 'Royal Scot' 4-6-0 No 46170 *British Legion*, with an afternoon express freight from Upperby yard to Willesden, pulls strongly away from Carlisle No 13 signalbox, where the goods lines from the various yards join the main line, in March 1962.

Below: Class 9F 2-10-0 No 92218 makes light work of the climb to Shap near Thrimby Grange with a heavy Carlisle to Crewe Basford Hall fitted freight in September 1967. The 9F 2-10-0s were only seen regularly over Shap in the last two years of BR steam.

Above: The last occasion I saw a 'Royal Scot' in active BR service — No 46115 *Scots Guardsman* leaves Plumpton loop with the 15.15 Carlisle yard to Crewe Basford Hall after being overtaken by the 12.20 Perth-Euston in October 1965.

Below: Returning home after overhaul at Cowlairs Works 'Black 5' No 45258 of Barrow depot takes advantage of the easing of the gradient past Southwaite with the Carlisle to Willesden perishable freight in September 1966. This train then carried the small number of milk tanks which formerly ran as a separate train. It is seen passing Southwaite loops, which were the first refuge out of Carlisle on the climb to Shap.

Above: The classic Shap scene. Class 5 45041 climbs strongly past Shap Wells with a Blackpool-Glasgow relief train on a misty autumn day in 1966.

Below: 'Lobster' 2-6-0 No 42954 of Springs Branch depot blasts past the site of the long closed Wreay station with a Carlisle yard to Crewe Basford Hall express freight in July 1965.

Right: The grimy surface of 'Britannia' Pacific No 70051 (formerly *Firth of Forth*) still reflects the early morning sunlight as the engine forges past Thrimby Grange with the 08.15 Carlisle to Crewe 'horse and carriage' parcels train in March 1967.

Above: 'Duchess' 4-6-2 No 46228 *Duchess of Rutland* forges through Wreay cutting with the Sunday afternoon milk express train from Carlisle to Mitre Bridge, London, in May 1964. This train picked up tanks from Appleby and Aspatria at Carlisle, then ran non-stop at express speeds to Milnthorpe, where further tanks were picked up. After this it called only at Crewe for crew changing.

Below: A woebegone 'Jubilee' from Warrington depot, No 45655 (formerly *Keith*), climbs away from Carlisle into the frosty February air with a Carlisle yard to Warrington freight in 1965. The garish diagonal yellow stripe prohibiting the engine from working 'under the wires' south of Crewe can be seen on the cab side.

Above: To celebrate the pleasant survival of the 'Lakes Express' into the 1965 summer Upperby turned out an especially clean engine to work the Penrith to Workington portion on the first occasion this train ran in June of that year. Here it is: Ivatt Class 2 2-6-0 No 46426 steps briskly away from Penrith at the start of the steep climb to Penruddock, made all the more difficult for these little engines by the need to slow for the single line tablet at Penrith No 1, right at the foot of the climb.

Below: Last struggles of steam over Shap. Class 5 No 44802 makes heavy weather of the twisting climb through Bessie Ghyll with a Summer Saturday Glasgow to Blackpool train in August 1967.

1Z12
45512

Left: Rebuilt 'Patriot' 4-6-0 No 45512 *Bunsen* struggles to keep its feet passing Carlisle No 13 signalbox with a Carlisle United football club supporters' charter train from Carlisle to Preston on 15 February 1964. On the right, Class 5 No 44691 waits on the goods lines to follow with a fitted freight.

Below left: One of the last two 'Royal Scots' in BR service, No 46140 makes heavy weather of the climb past Wreay with the afternoon Carlisle yard to Willesden perishables train in April 1965.

Below: On a golden July evening in 1965, Class 5 No 45112 hurries through Penrith with a down express goods. The cloud-covered Westmorland fells can be seen in the background.

Above: As 'Patriot' 4-6-0 No 45551 thrashed past Shap Wells amidst a rain of cinders with the Saturdays only 13.20 Euston to Glasgow in July 1958 the driver and certainly the fireman seemed to be regretting not stopping at Tebay for a banker. This train, which was formed of the weekday 'Caledonian' eight-coach set plus a few strengthening coaches, was usually the preserve of a Pacific; to get a 'Patriot' was quite unusual. It is interesting to note the complete absence of steam leakage despite the dirty condition and the hard working of the engine.

Below: Stranger on Shap. *Flying Scotsman*'s Gresley 3-cylinder beat echoes around the Westmorland hills as he makes a determined assault on Shap. Seen here at Greenholme with a North Eastern Locomotive Preservation Group sponsored railtour from Newcastle to Keighley, which returned via Carlisle. This train, bearing an LNER-type headboard 'The North Eastern', ran in May 1968.

Above: 'Britannia' Pacific No 70014 *Iron Duke* hurries the 14.00 Glasgow to Liverpool along the Lune Valley at 70-80mph with steam to spare. Seen in July 1967, the engine is fitted with a high-sided, coal pusher-fitted tender removed from one of his withdrawn brothers in the 70045-54 range.

Below: In the light and shade of a 1967 August evening, 'Britannia' Pacific No 70028 (formerly *Royal Star*) takes a run at Shap with the Carlisle portion of the 11.00 from Euston — at that time the successor of the 'Lakes Express'. Seen here in the Lune Valley, now transformed by the M6 motorway, which closely follows the railway on the right of the picture.

Above: Now to the Midland route south from Carlisle. Clan Pacific No 72008 *Clan Macleod* does its utmost to get the Easter Monday 1963 relief to the 'Thames-Clyde Express' on the move past the old Midland engine sheds at Durran Hill, Carlisle.

Below: Looking very out of place, GWR 'Castle' class 4-6-0 No 7029 *Clun Castle* takes advantage of the easier grades past Armathwaite with a railtour returning over Ais Gill to Preston on a mellow September evening in 1967.

Above: A one-time Kingmoor 'Crab' 2-6-0 No 42831, by then exiled at the GC Gorton shed, makes a welcome and noteworthy return to its old haunts with the 13.04 Carlisle to Skipton Class 8 freight on 15 February 1964.

Below: Typical Midland main line power. 'Jubilee' 4-6-0 No 45697 *Achilles*, by now painted in unlined green, nameless and disfigured by a yellow stripe, makes a brave showing on the initial climb out of Carlisle past Cumwhinton with the 'CTAC Holiday Tours Express' from Gourock to Leicester on 7 August 1965.

44675

Left: Class 5 4-6-0 No 44675 makes a savage attack on the climb to Ais Gill with a Carlisle Yard to Margam fitted freight which had been diverted owing to motorway bridge construction on the Shap route in April 1967. Photographed south of Kirkby Stephen.

Above: Faithful Midland Railway veteran 0-6-0 No 43960 chatters along past Duncowfold with the 13.04 Carlisle to Skipton, by now upgraded to Class 7 status, in August 1964. Note the tender cab fitted to the Skipton and Hellifield members of this class for snowplough duty on the wild, exposed parts of the Ais Gill route.

Below: 'Jubilee' 4-6-0 No 45626 *Seychelles* ably deputises for a failed diesel on an afternoon express goods up the Midland line and is seen here attacking the first rise at 1 in 131 out of Carlisle past Cumwhinton in September 1964.

Above: Ais Gill summit is in sight for Class 9F No 92096 as it makes light work of the Long Meg to Widnes Anhydrite train, towards sunset on a stormy February afternoon in 1966.

Below: A not so hackneyed view of the Shap gradient. Class 9F No 92076 coasts down the incline towards Greenholme with 5M27, the Larbert to Wallerscoate soda ash empties, an ICI charter train, in August 1967.

Right: On the last mile of the climb to Ais Gill summit 'Jubilee' 4-6-0 No 45626 *Seychelles* is not having a happy time with the 09.43 Carlisle Yard to Stourton fitted freight. The heavy load of concrete sleepers and steel castings has brought her almost to a stand as she struggles to keep moving on a dull June day in 1965.

45626

44125

Left: The only other route south from Carlisle is the former Maryport & Carlisle line to Workington connecting with the Furness railway to Barrow. It is not a very photogenic route as it runs along the flat Solway Coastal plain. Here is Class 4F 0-6-0 No 44125 crossing the River Caldew at Cummersdale with the evening Carlisle yard to Workington freight in August 1964.

Above: Ex-works Class 5 No 44983 makes light work of the last few yards to Ais Gill as she blots out Wild Boar Fell in August 1964 with the 12.40 Carlisle to Stourton express freight.

Below: The battle is over for 'Crab' 2-6-0 No 42787 and its crew as they commence the long downhill run from Ais Gill to Carlisle with a down Midland line partially fitted freight in July 1963.

75051

Left: The Skipton 4F 0-6-0s were replaced in 1965 by BR Class 4 4-6-0s. Here No 75051 approaches the mini-summit at mp 300 near Cotehill. This was the first 'breather' for trains climbing from Carlisle, in much the same way as Southwaite on the LNW route.

Above: BR's official last steam train, the iniquitous 15-guinea special, makes its way up the pastoral Eden Valley to Ais Gill on 11 August 1968. The two engines — Class 5 4-6-0s Nos 44871 and 44781 — were very appropriate to this magnificent route.

Below: The fireman can be seen through the cab window bending his back to satisfy the appetite of Class 5 No 45112 as she makes steady progress up the last mile of the Ais Gill climb with the 12.40 Carlisle to Stourton fitted freight. Although this shot was taken in February 1966, the clement weather was unusual, as witnessed by the snowplough on the engine.

Above: 'Duchess' Pacific No 46238 *City of Carlisle* makes a steady start out of its namesake with the Sunday 13.00 meat train to Broad Street in December 1963.

Below: 'Jinties' were always part of the Carlisle scene. Here 0-6-0T No 47326 heads for Citadel station with empty coaching stock from Upperby Carriage sidings in June 1965.

Above: Rebuilt 'Patriot' No 45545 *Planet* starts cautiously out of Carlisle Citadel station with a football excursion to Workington on Boxing Day 1963.

Below: 'Royal Scot' 4-6-0 No 46136 *The Border Regiment* leaves Carlisle with a Glasgow to Manchester express in March 1963.

Above: 'Britannia' 4-6-2 No 70018 *Flying Dutchman* attacks the steep rise to Canal Junction past Carlisle No 1 signalbox with the 13.28 Carlisle to Edinburgh stopping train in February 1962. The 'Britannias' replaced the A3 Pacifics at Canal shed on Waverley route duties, but their reign was short-lived. The constant curvature of this sinuous route caused them all to be despatched to Crewe works with loose tyres within a few months and 'Black 5s' took over with more success.

Below: Class 2 2-6-0s No 46458 and 46434 stand in Carlisle's platform 3 at the head of 'The Great Cumberland Railroad Rave', a special train for jazz enthusiasts run from Carlisle to Bassenthwaite Lake by Carlisle Jazz Club. The train was formed of five coaches, which in the event were unused, and five parcels vans fitted out as dance halls with bars, groups etc. It ran to Bassenthwaite Lake station where it was stabled for several hours while the dancing continued, returning to Carlisle on the Sunday evening.

Above: 'Crab' 2-6-0 No 42854 sets out from Carlisle Citadel with the 16.20 stopping train to Preston on a Sunday in April 1956.

Below: Class A4 4-6-2 No 60027 *Merlin* branches away from the West Coast main line at Port Carlisle Junction with a railtour returning to Edinburgh over the Waverley route in June 1965. This ex-North British Railway line branched from the Caledonian in a westerly direction, turned north at Canal Junction, crossed the Eden on its own bridge just north of this junction and then finally achieved its north-easterly direction at Stainton crossing over the CR main line just north of Kingmoor, between the shed and the new marshalling yard.

Above: Fairburn 2-6-4T No 42095 heads west from Carlisle along the Solway Firth with a Sunday Silloth train in August 1962. This branch was converted from a canal, as can be seen from the formation, and this is how Carlisle Canal shed got its name. This view shows the train accelerating away from Canal Junction, where the Silloth branch left the Waverley Route.

Below: Before the concentration of all freight operation in Carlisle at Kingmoor, Class 4F 0-6-0 No 44305 approaches Upperby Yard with a transfer trip from London Road yard, while Class 5 45435 prepares to set out for the South with a freight from Upperby yard.

Above: Edinburgh (Haymarket) Class A1 Pacific No 60161 *North British* eases the 13.57 Class 5 freight out of Canal Yard at the start of its journey to Millerhill via Hawick in April 1961.

Below: 'Britannia' Pacific No 70051 *Firth of Forth* tops up with water at Upperby shed prior to working the 16.00 milk express to Willesden in April 1960. Pacific No 46256 *Sir William A. Stanier F.R.S.* is behind as main line stand-by.

Above: In 1963 the commissioning of the vast marshalling yard at Kingmoor caused the transfer of all freight working to the nearby motive power depot. Kingmoor was thus a very busy and important depot, as evidenced by this view taken in 1965 on a Sunday. By this time the ex-LNER types from the Waverley route were being serviced here, and thus a B1 and V2 can be seen in this view. We see here the north end of the depot.

Below: In earlier days Carlisle was served by numerous railways, each with its own engine sheds. In BR times these had shrunk to three full depots — Canal (ex-NBR); Kingmoor (ex-CR); and Upperby (ex-LNWR). On 16 June 1963 Canal closed and its duties were divided amongst the other two. Here is a view of the depot, from the coal stage, on the penultimate Sunday. Formerly an LNER shed, its transfer in 1958 to the London Midland region — Code 12C — from the Scottish Region saw the replacement of its A3 Pacifics and B1 4-6-0s and various other ex-LNER types by ex-LMS and standard designs. Ex-LNER types were still serviced here in 1963 after working in over the Waverley route from Edinburgh. Amongst the engines visible in this view are A4 No 60012, A3 No 60100, V2 No 60816, B1 No 61099 and 'Britannia' No 70020.

Above right: 'Britannia' Pacific No 70003 rests at Kingmoor in 1966.

Below right: On a busy Summer Saturday in 1966, four 'Black Fives' — Nos 44820 and 44881 both from Motherwell, No 44998 from Perth and No 44878 of Kingmoor — await their next turn of duty in the light and airy Kingmoor running shed.

70003

44881
44998
44878

Above left: One of the last active 'Patriots', No 45531 *Sir Frederick Harrison*, awaits its next turn of duty inside Kingmoor running shed.

Left: 'Britannia' Pacific No 70031 *Byron* has his smokebox raked out at Upperby after arrival at Carlisle with a parcels train from the South in December 1964.

Above: Boiler washout at Kingmoor, 1967.

Above right: The south end of Kingmoor in 1960, showing entirely ex-LMS power.

Right: Class A1 Pacific No 60161 *North British* and 'Duchess' 4-6-2 No 46244 *King George VI* come face to face at Kingmoor in 1964. *King George VI* was waiting to work the 20.25 passenger to Perth and *North British* the 21.32 freight to Aberdeen Craiginches via the Waverley route.

KING GEORGE VI

Left: A rear end view of what I consider to have been Britain's most handsome steam locomotive — a maroon 'Princess Royal' No 46200 at Kingmoor in 1962.

Below: Preparatory to working a freight over the Waverley route to Edinburgh, Class V2 2-6-2 No 60816 is turned on the Kingmoor turntable. The open space in the background was the site of the ex-CR Kingmoor marshalling yard and is now occupied by the Carlisle diesel depot. It will be noticed that the engine is being turned by hand — a frequent occurrence due to the failure of the vacuum-operated turning mechanism.

Right: The high-speed climb over Shap has evidently been too much for *Clun Castle's* draughting arrangements, judging by the accumulation of ash in the smokebox. The Kingmoor disposal crew smile grimly as this unpleasant surprise meets them when they open the door in September 1967.

Below: 'Clan' 4-6-2 No 72007 and Fairburn 2-6-4T No 42052 stand side by side at Kingmoor on a cold windy February day in 1966. The 2-6-4T was returning home to Holbeck Leeds after overhaul at Cowlairs Works in Glasgow.

46200

46230
DUCHESS OF BUCCLEUCH

Above left: Pride of Kingmoor — 'Princess Royal' 4-6-2 No 46200 leaves the shed to work the 18.00 Sunday Parcels to Perth in the summer of 1962.

Left: Pride of Polmadie — 'Duchess' Pacific No 46230 *Duchess of Buccleuch* is posed for me as she leaves Kingmoor shed to return home on the Sunday 'Royal Scot' in April 1960.

Above: North of Carlisle both sets of lines cross the River Eden by means of Etterby Bridge. Here 'Clan' 4-6-2 No 72008 *Clan Macleod* restarts from a signal stop in foggy conditions with the 11.00 Carlisle to Glasgow St. Enoch stopping train. A Class 5 approaches over the goods lines on the right. Taken in November 1964.

Below: Clan Pacific No 72005 *Clan Macgregor* bustles through the closed Gretna Green station with the 11.00 Carlisle to Glasgow St Enoch stopping train in February 1965.

Bottom: As the main lines from Carlisle to the north pass Kingmoor engine sheds, the chord from the Waverley route joins from the west. This short line was constructed in 1963 to enable freight trains to use the ex-NBR goods lines from the South to Canal, cross the Eden on the bridge there and then regain access to the new marshalling yard from the CR goods lines. Here Class 4 2-6-0 No 43040 heads for the marshalling yard with parcels vans from the Citadel station, followed under permissive block working by Class 5 No 44998 and B1 No 61099, which were to work northbound freights from the yard. Taken on 1 November 1965 — a day of Carlisle's heaviest snowfall for years.

Right: In wintry weather 'Britannia' Pacific No 70041 sets out from Carlisle yard with the 12.46 freight for Warrington on 1 November 1965.

Below right: A few minutes after the lower shot on the facing page, Class 5 4-6-0 No 44986 approaches the yard and is about to pass under the Waverley route with a Class 8 freight from Wigan which has been routed over the NB goods lines and the chord line. The up 'Royal Scot' speeds into Carlisle behind a Brush Type 4 diesel on the main line and in the background an English Electric Type 1 approaches over the ex-CR goods lines with a train of limestone from the Hardendale Quarry at Shap.

Above: 'Britannia' Pacific No 70049 *Solway Firth* hurries north past Rockcliffe — by coincidence the point on the West Coast main line where it is nearest to the engine's namesake — with the Sunday 9.30 Manchester/Liverpool to Edinburgh/Glasgow in November 1964.

Below: 'Jubilee' 4-6-0 No 45660 *Rooke* heads north out of Carlisle on 7 August 1965 with the summer Saturday 09.30 from St. Pancras to Glasgow. This train was a relief to the 'Thames-Clyde Express' and would fork left at Gretna Junction to follow the ex-Glasgow & South Western route to Glasgow via Dumfries and Kilmarnock. The Waverley route can be seen diverging away to the right, crossing the ex-CR goods lines, which have by-passed the passenger station via Dentonholme.

Above right: 'Britannia' Pacific No 70038 works hard to accelerate the heavy 12.30 Sunday Carlisle to Glasgow parcels up the gradient from Gretna Junction through Gretna Green on the ex-G&SW route in December 1965.

Below right: 'Britannia' Pacific No 70016 *Ariel* heads north through a wintry Solway landscape at Rockcliffe with the 12.30 Sunday Carlisle to Glasgow parcels, which would diverge left on to the G&SW route at Gretna Junction. Taken in November 1965.

70038

Above: 'Jubilee' 4-6-0 No 45635 *Tobago* with the Sunday 18.00 Carlisle to Perth parcels is unusually routed over the goods lines on the western perimeter of the huge Carlisle marshalling yard in August 1964 due to Sunday permanent way work on the main line, which runs on the eastern side of the yard.

Below: Rebuilt 'Patriot' 4-6-0 No 45512 *Bunsen* lays a smoke screen over the site of Britain's worst rail accident at Quintinshill as it eases for a pw restriction with the 09.30 Manchester/Liverpool to Edinburgh/Glasgow in September 1964. The signalbox, scene of the tragic sequence of events early on a 1915 morning, is lost in the smoke haze behind the down main line home signal, seen here in the off position.

Above: 'Jubilee' 4-6-0 No 45567 *South Australia* passes Upperby with an afternoon express freight from Crewe to Carlisle Yard on an August evening in 1964. It has been routed over the goods lines, by means of which it will bypass the Citadel passenger station and reach the marshalling yard. The two lines at the extreme right-hand side form the West Coast main line.

Below: Standard Class 5 No 73107 climbs strongly up Beattock bank past Greskine refuge siding with a block load of coal for Scottish industry, assisted in the rear by a Class 4 2-6-0. The coach at the front was used to transport railway families to and from their isolated cottages at Beattock summit; known as the "Siege of Beattock", it usually ran on Saturdays only and was ferried up and down by a banking engine from Beattock depot. On this occasion however, Whit Saturday 1966, there was no path available in the heavy traffic for such a working and the coach was attached to the front of this freight.

46203

'Princess Royal' swan song. Pacific No 46203 *Princess Margaret Rose* makes a steady climb up Beattock bank past Harthope with the 10.10 Euston to Perth express in August 1962. This was the last passenger run of this fine locomotive. When it returned to Kingmoor the following day on an afternoon fish working from Perth it was withdrawn from service.

Left: The syncopated three-cylinder exhaust beat of Class V2 No 60964 echoes over Brampton Fell as it climbs strongly towards the Tyne Eden watershed past Heads Nook with the Summer Saturdays Stranraer to Newcastle train on 24 July 1963.

Below: Although almost all the car-carrying trains from the Midlands car factories to the Bathgate terminal were diesel-hauled, the 10.15 Saturdays only Ford train from Ditton Junction (Halewood) was an exception. South of Carlisle it was usually worked by a Class 5 or 9F, but for the difficult gradients and curves of the Waverley route its 20 or 22 bogie load needed double-heading. Many permutations of Classes A3, A4, V2, B1, Class 5 were seen and here is one. 'Black 5' No 44672 and A4 No 60024 *Kingfisher* battle with a strong west wind as they climb up past Stainton Junction to the bridge over the West Coast main line at Kingmoor in April 1964.

Above right: Immediately after crossing the Eden B1 No 61244 *Strang Steel* and V2 No 60824 take a run at the rise past Stainton Junction up to the bridge over the West Coast main line with the 10.15 SO Ditton Junction-Bathgate Ford liner car train in September 1964. The siding on the right is the connection from Carlisle marshalling yard enabling northbound freight trains to reach the Waverley route from the departure yard, a manoeuvre which involved the engine running round its train by means of the connection seen in this picture.

Below right: Another shot of the 10.15 Ditton Junction to Bathgate, seen here in desolate country near Riccarton. Class 5 No 44883 and the unique V2 with stovepipe chimney and shovel-shaped smoke deflector, No 60813, are seen at grips with the long 1 in 75 climb from Newcastleton to Whitrope summit.

Above: Class B1 4-6-0 No 61395 leaves Hexham with the 15.12 express to Newcastle in 1958. The B1s maintained by the Scottish Region were distinguishable by the fact that curved pieces of metal were welded into the footplating below the cab and above the cylinders to soften the angle; this feature can be seen here.

Below: Class V2 No 60824 makes light work of the short 11.15 Carlisle to Millerhill Class D freight in July 1965. It is seen here passing Riccarton Junction — the legendary isolated railway community accessible only by rail and situated in the heart of the Border fells. By this time the meandering Border Counties Branch to Hexham had been closed for eight years; its engine shed was demolished as banking engines were no longer taken by northbound trains for the 10 mile climb from Newcastleton to Whitrope summit, up which Riccarton was about three-quarters of the way. Only the lonely signalbox was still in use — all the houses in the "village" were unoccupied.

Above: Before disfiguration by double chimney or 'elephant's ears', Class A3 No 60093 *Coronach* makes a brisk start from Hexham with the 14.00 Carlisle to Newcastle express in March 1958.

Below: Class K1 2-6-0 No 62007, specially loaned from Sunderland depot, climbs the long 1 in 107 through How Mill with an LCGB Manchester to Carlisle-Newcastle to Manchester railtour in late Autumn 1966. The K1 was used for the Carlisle to Newcastle stretch.

Above: A B1 pays a visit to the West Coast main line. No 61357 plods homeward through Kirkpatrick Fleming with the 13.00 Carlisle Yard to Millerhill in March 1964.

Below: Class B1 No 61099 seems to be making unduly hard work of the featherweight 18.13 Carlisle to Hawick local as it hurries through Steele Road without stopping in June 1965. In fact there was not one passenger on the train as it passed me, which rather confirmed BR's decision to close the Waverley route.

Above: Border passing place. Class V1 2-6-2T No 67606 on a St Boswells-bound passenger train overtakes Class J39 0-6-0 No 64917 on the branch freight at Kelso, midway along the Tweedmouth to St Boswells line in May 1958.

Below: BR Class 4 2-6-0 No 76070 takes a rest from its weekday duty as a Beattock banker to work an engineer's train in connection with deep drainage of the West Coast main line in preparation for the continuous welded rail programme and ultimate electrification. Here it is seen creeping out of Quintinshill loop following the passage of the Sunday Manchester to Glasgow train in autumn 1965.

Above: Class A3 Pacific No 60100 *Spearmint* blasts through Riccarton Junction with the 14.12 Class 8 freight from Carlisle yard to Millerhill in August 1965.

Below: Class B1 No 61324 climbs smartly through Twizell en route from Tweedmouth to Jedburgh with a Border branches railtour on Easter Sunday 1964.

Above: On the line connecting Newcastle and Carlisle, Class B16 4-6-0 No 61459 leaves Hexham on a golden summer Saturday evening in 1959 with the Stranraer to Newcastle through train. This engine, allocated to Selby depot, was running-in from Darlington works and was presumably appropriated by Gateshead to alleviate the usual summer Saturday engine shortage of those days.

Below: An interestingly powered railtour seen here leaving Wennington tunnel on the Carnforth-Hellifield branch of the ex-Midland railway. BR Class 4 4-6-0s Nos 75019 and 75027 return south with a railtour from the steam-starved metropolis in June 1968.

60083

Above: LNER visitor on Beattock. Heaton Class A3 No 60083 *Sir Hugo* was most surprisingly rostered by Kingmoor to work the 10.10 Euston to Perth north from Carlisle one Saturday in July 1964. She is seen here at Harthope making light work of the climb, admittedly with a very modest load.

Left: Beattock banker, April 1965.

Right: 'Clan' Pacific No 72006 (formerly *Clan Mackenzie*) attacks the 1 in 75 past Creetown with a Stranraer to Woodburn troop special in May 1965, only a month before the closure of this wild, desolate and unremunerative line.

Above: Class 5 No 45432 and 'Clan' Pacific No 72007 climb the 1 in 75 from Dumfries to Lochanhead with a 10coach Woodburn to Stranraer troop train on 30 May 1965, two weeks before the closure of the Dumfries-Stranraer line.

Below: Class 2P 4-4-0 No 40654 makes an unusual combination with a Fairburn 2-6-4T leaving Ravenglass with a Workington to Manchester stopping train in September 1957.